Why? The Reason of Existence & the Meaning of Everything

Tareq Alhindi

Warning!

We will be discussing several existential questions that may have been avoided by most of us, from the simplest question to the most mentally demanding. This may change your understanding of life and human activities. But remember! We are trying to investigate the meaning behind everything, not in any way to undermine or look down upon such human activities or people's lifestyle.

On the individual level, contemplating these questions go through three stages, starting with the stage of 'No Questioning', which results in an illusory state of comfort. The second stage is 'Excess Questioning', which causes mental fatigue, just like a bodybuilder lifting heavy weights to become stronger, you ask to become wiser. The last stage can lead you into two paths, the first path leads you back to the 'No Questioning' stage, where you seek that illusionary comfort again, avoiding any deep mental stimulation. The second path leads you to depression or to pseudo-wisdom, and you might lose interest in life, since you are not able to get the answers for all these questions or for being unable to comprehend the answers.

But falling into depression is wrong! Becoming a nihilist is just an easy escape, it's the choice of those who have pseudo-wisdom and we shall see why. I kindly ask you to continue your journey, don't give up and surrender, depression might be a phase that will soon pass, and pseudo-wisdom is a state that can be cured. For the results of walking the inquisition path are quite satisfying, where the meanings behind everything will be unveiled (if not all then most), and with that comes true happiness and satisfaction, which can never be matched by any other thing.

Please read all the book, it is a one piece (that's why there is no table of contents, and I tried to keep it short), and please don't prejudge based on partial information or any prior socio-historical influence. Then if you finish reading please contemplate a lot, and remember to keep emotions away from logic.

I hope it will be a useful reading for you.

Also, I would like to apologize for using the pronoun 'he' often, I am for gender equality and more than that, but I refrained from using 'she/he' in the book. Now you can think of me referring to the old 'me' when I use 'he', I hope that suffice as an excuse.

I wish you all happiness and success in achieving the answer for the most important question 'WHY?'

Introduction

This book is different.
Here we go again!

How many time we have heard these words before?
This book is different, this movie is different and this philosophy is different...

But truly, without being arrogant or rude, without complications or oversimplification, this book showcases human activities and reasoning briefly and to the point. No lies, no cosmetics, no material gain, no ethical, political or religious agenda, no fantasy, no cheesy conclusions nor dreamy motivational statements.

Just naked reality, a description of what 'it' 'is' (or always 'was' or 'will'!), no racial or national distinctions or any other reasonable or unreasonable divisions. No beautification for the reality when it shows its "ugly" face. This book is about the human phenomenon (as intelligent beings), about our actions regardless of our level of ignorance.

Ignorance!

Why not "our knowledge"?
That is why the book title is "WHY?"

As human beings, what do we really know? For what is
dominant in human societies is ignorance, which might
improve sometimes (for some) and reach the state of
knowing that you don't know, hence becoming a knowledge
seeker, searching for wisdom, a philosopher. Ignorance is
rather too strong of a term, but I used it to stress our state of
lacking ultimate truth, we doubt then we believe.

As for the ultimate wisdom (truth) itself…
Oooh! Wisdom.

I don't know if any human -or any other intelligent being-
has ever gained the complete and perfect wisdom!

By the way, I'm not melancholic nor a pessimist, on the
contrary, I am super optimistic, at least I ask using "why" and
what an achievement is this!

Blah blah blah!

Enough with the introduction, let's start…
Just a moment, please!

So briefly, we will showcase key human actions and
discuss principles that we consider as defining for what does
it mean to be wise human beings (Homo sapiens), and after
presenting the naked reality we will try to extract the
meanings, the answers and the telos -if there is any- of every
existence.

The book is quite short, I do apologies for the assumption that might arise that I am not arguing enough about certain points, but I am not running away from debate, it is me showing that the logic presented was enough to clarify and justify my explanation.

> For when the rhetoric is not concise
> It is like using too much spice

The Power of the Question & the Anathema of Ignorance

My eyes are open, but I can't see!
I hear, but I don't understand!
Where am I? In what time? Time! But what is time?
What are these sounds that I'm making?
Are they dangerous? Who's that holding me?
The voices have stopped! What happened?
I feel safe… Comfortable…
In what world am I?
What am I?
Why am I?
Why?

As if they are leftovers of some distant memories! Memories from the moments my mother gave birth to me and I came forth into this world.

The human cometh to this life with no information, but he has the tools to help him gain knowledge, an underdeveloped sight, you hear but you don't understand, all these sensors for temperature, texture, orientation, smell and taste. All sensing the world for the first time, and we still don't know how to manage the control panel (the brain).

You grow up and the years pass by, you ask some simple questions with no deep contemplation. Investigating what's around you.

You hold things, then you try to put them in your mouth, you shake them… then you throw them away!

You are at school now, you learned how to talk a few years ago and now you can read, you learn by example, by knowledge transfer from those who came before. Oh! And now you can do your first pure logical thinking by solving some mathematical problems $(1+1+1=3)$.

Your questions have increased, where did the clouds come from? How are candies made? Where did my grandpa go? Where do babies come from? Why you don't like me asking?

You became more serious, more dangerous, you started to contemplate the answers.

Few years ago, if your parents told you that giants live above the clouds you would've believed it. But now after you have studied science, you know it's impossible, it was just a lie. Clouds are water vapor and some dust, it is gaseous (an aerosol to be more precise), plus there is no enough concentration of oxygen at that altitude to sustain human life, let alone giants. Oh! Wait…Giants!

That surely made you question the reliability of your source of information (I hope!)

Here you are now, had finished your undergraduate studies, and followed it with the graduate studies…But!

You were thinking that you will get the answers for those questions…

For all the questions!

The same questions that started with you since you came to this life:

Where did we come from? Why do we continue living? Why there is life? Why the good and evil? Or why there is a universe to start with?

But it seems that the questions remained unanswered. And to make it worse! Each one of those questions gave rise to millions of new questions, as if it is a little spark that popped in a dry hay field, igniting it and all that's around! Until there was no place in this universe that is left safe from this flame!

But flames can be a painful destructive force or a benevolent warmth and illumination (from our human perspective).

The Questions

Since quite an early age, I tried to understand the paradigm of human knowledge. I tried to make a system about the science of questioning things -later I discovered philosophy ☺ - and I noticed that there are five elements of existence in our universe:

1. Space: so we ask using 'where', to get the knowledge of the place or relative position.
2. Time: so we ask using 'when', to get the knowledge of the order of accidents.
3. Movement: so we ask using 'how' and 'what', to get the knowledge of the form and modality.
4. Count: so we ask using 'how many', so we got calculus or mathematics.
   And the most difficult and important is:
5. Reason: so we ask using 'why', to get the meaning, the cause and telos of every existence.

So if you acquire the answers for all these questions, you will get the complete knowledge, the ultimate truth about everything. You will be truly wise.

The first four questions are the domain of the natural sciences, engineering and mathematics. The science of tangible things, which is limited by our ability to sense and analyze the universe around us, which paves the way for the answer to the fifth question 'Why?'.

For knowing the reason is the domain of philosophy (as we shall see later), knowing why is what makes an intelligent being truly wise, it is the knowledge beyond tangible things, it is the ability to comprehend absolute ideas, to understand the purpose or the telos.

'Why' is the domain of the true ego, the 'I' that stands behind the control panel, some people might call it the soul, others prefer a more materialistic friendly term such as 'consciousness', or you can call it as in the famous Japanese movie the 'Ghost in the Shell', named after 'The Ghost in the Machine' for Arthur Koestler discussing the mind–body problem (more on that later). Whatever you prefer, for now let's go with self-consciousness, that what makes you realize that you are you, and not someone else. Which I believe every sane human agrees on, hence we use words such as: I, you and them.

There is a pleasure in knowing, a satisfaction when answering questions, but as soon you answer one question you realize that there are many more ahead, more difficult and more elusive.

It is not wise to generalize -sorry!- but most people try to live their lives with the minimum amount of pondering these annoying existential questions, and they tend to accept the simplest of answers even without being certain about it, just to have a sense of relief and control, an illusionary peace of mind as we mentioned before.

They wake up in the morning, they take a shower, they eat, go to work, get some money, some social contacts guided -mainly- by materialistic self-interest and some psychological tendencies toward being in a herd or a family (safety in number, etc.). They reproduce, they take care of the products 'the kids' (at least most of them do!). More and more human beings! They grow old, they senesce, then they die...

And then!
Oh!
Was that living?
Just like any other plant or animal on this planet!

Now I am not criticizing their life style, our lifestyle, or life itself. Since I cannot be alive and choose not to eat, I don't choose to get sick, I will definitely need your help and the existence of a human society around me. These are basic needs, requirements to stay alive. What bothers me are not the actions, but the meaning behind each action.

I am not worried about getting a job, having friends or starting or maintaining a family. Nor I am worried about not getting sick or living in peace here or there. Not even bothered by the fact that I'll die someday.

Not any of that bothers me! The thing that fills my mind all the time is the question 'Why?'

Why all these creatures continue on living? Why a lower life form in our eyes, like a bug or even a freaking sponge just setting at the bottom of the ocean choose to live? Does it choose to live? Why they reproduce? I will not be here after sometime, so why should I care to leave a legacy or whatever?

Why should I care if in the future the earth will explode or the universe will cease to exist?

Why single cell organisms like bacteria keep on living? Why does a bacterium divide? It does not have a brain to choose, so is it just automatic? Is it a slavery to the laws of physics? What if all the living things on earth decided to die? Just realized that there is no point in struggling for life! No point of being a slave for these physical laws!

In a grand cosmic nihilistic revolution.
Now that will be a grand manifestation of true freedom.
An escape from all binding laws, of this cosmic slavery.
But is that even possible?

Maybe that's why scientists can't find that advanced alien civilization!

I am not sure about bacteria, but at least we humans are smart enough to contemplate such existential questions! But is there really no point to all of it 'life'?

Some might say the motivation for living is personal, maybe animals enjoy being alive! Plants too! Well, at least I doubt that bacteria have feelings, because if they do, this opens the door for bigger questions.

For a moment let's say it's the enjoyment that maintain our will to live, then why reproduction? After our death, there is no meaning of having many or zero children. Why doesn't a tree keep on growing, taking all the space and resources for itself? The same goes for that first living cell, why didn't it has all the planet for itself? Why losing energy on producing flowers and seeds, why division! So the new copies come to existence and compete with it for space and resources, and might be the reason of its struggle and demise. I'm sure the first cell wasn't feeling lonely!

Again, is life a byproduct of physics? Is it an automatic process? No choice or free well here to be found! For many organisms, I might agree, but what about us, humans! Am I not already questioning and repelling against these laws now.

I wake up in the morning...
So! Why should I live today?
Why to continue existing?

Under the shower, I think... Here we go again with this demanding body of mine, you have to clean it, to take care of it, not to break it or get it damaged by injury or infection.

But why?

Indeed being sick isn't pleasant thing, I don't want to feel any pain! Well, this is an answer for the "primitive why".

Food! Food! Food!

That routine is going to drive me crazy! That heavy need, every living organism must eat, have a source of energy, and I must add another living body to my own to keep on living!

An animal, a plant it doesn't matter! Find it! Kill it! And if you want to appear civilized then cook it! Then add it to your body.

Everyday...
As long as you are alive.

That is why I don't understand the hypocrisy of being a vegan. All living things are equally alive! But suddenly it's ok to kill a plant, or worse! Put it a life in the oven with some living yeast cells, burn them! Then eat your vegetarian pizza pie.

I do understand the cruelty in the meat industry, but did you "forget" how many billions of poor little bugs had to die to get you the wheat for your pizza dough?

Or get an infection, and your body will do the killing for millions of poor little single cell organisms. The point is, whether you wish it or not, there will be blood.

Why?

Well, I said, I can't choose not to eat and stay alive. Some people enjoy food, others just want to survive. But again these are answers to the primitive why.

But really, why we must eat each other? I know plants survive by photosynthesis "+", thanks for noticing! But let's consider slavery to sunlight is similar to slavery to other source of energy sources in other organisms, the question remains the same. Why we waste most of our time filling our tummies? Processing information while transferring energy! Is that life?

Why we have been created to need food or any external energy source? Or was it just another inevitable outcome of the physical laws?

We go out for work, it's true that we can gain some money or even just fill our time with something other than eating, but aren't we filling another void! A mental void!

Socializing, getting in contact with other humans. As I said, most of us are seeking a materialistic or some psychological gain.

We go back home and now we eat again, we defecate, we sleep, we breathe, we dream! Then we wake up the next morning asking the same questions, and repeating the same routine.

And as societies we just keep reproducing ourselves. You struggle to study, to get a job, to have a house, to get accepted in your community. The bigger the community the harder the struggle is, and only when you start to "fail" in doing this routine you get angry and sad! And suddenly all these questions you've been running away from attack you again.

The irony is, on the other side of the spectrum, that person who has plenty of money, a "comfortable" life, that who has friends and family, he travelled, he had fun and literally have done all the possible things to be done on this planet (or any other). You usually find him bored, angry or sad, he might even get depressed and commit suicide! For there is nothing left to do! Why to keep on living then? At least those who never have done these activities seek to have the first time experience, but do it again and again... And it turns into a routine, a boring, heavy, meaningless, mechanical routine.

For the pleasure is in the fantasy, in dreaming to have, or do something. But once the perfect image in fantasy manifests as a distorted version in reality, or even manifests perfectly as your dream was, it loses its value.

But then why we continue?
Same events in history only with different names.
I am really bored of these human actions...And the actions of animals, plants and all other organisms.

It's all the same routine!

I am sick of us pretending to know it all, I am sick of our inability to comprehend.

I am bored of eating, drinking and even breathing.

I am sick of us fighting each other, how stupid are we? When will humanity's autoimmune disease be cured? Well it be cured? You fight to dominate the world! OK, you own the whole planet now! One world government or one nation or whatever! How boring!

I am sick of masters and slaves, like there is a difference!

I am sick of the laws and norms that stupid people came up with in the distant past, and up until this moment.

I am sick of us pretending to be civilized, I am sick of us copying each other, of being obsessed with the actions of the other. Again, as if we are different!

It is the same routine, wherever you look at, you will find nothing new.

I am bored of poverty and of wealth.

I am bored of all those who speaks from behind podiums, in squares and on screens, or even through books.

I am bored of work and of unemployment.

I am sick of masculine this and feminize that, of she/he/xe, or any crazy classification they are coming up with these days.

I am sick of advertisements and of fashion, of technology and of environment. I am sick of consumerism and of any damn retro-naturalism.

I am bored of us acting like we really care.

I am bored of listening and of speaking too.

Yet!

I am not a pessimist nihilist, nor an optimistic mystic, nor a materialistic pragmatic, nor an ignorant conformist.

Simply, I am an intelligent human being who want to know the absolute holistic ultimate truth.

Until few years ago, a visit to a new city in a new country used to bring joy to me, but soon I realized that suffocating routine was everywhere!

All the cities are the same, houses, cars, shops and people eating, sleeping and reproducing. The same actions all around.

I ran away from the present to the past, I went to museums, but alas! I found the same routine. Spoons, knives, plates, swords, houses and palaces. Damn!

I ran away to art galleries, thinking I might find an escape route in the fantasy world! Paintings, statues… Wait a minute! They depict people eating, sleeping, fighting, reproducing…
Damn!

Let's go beyond reality, surreal art! Interesting at the first look, but wait a minute! It's just a distorted reality, another failed attempt to escape the routine.

Where to go then? Why this universal routine? Why we keep repeating the same routine that millions have done before us and millions will keep repeating it in the future?

As a wise man once said: "history repeats itself because nobody was listening the first time". Well I think my friend that history repeats itself because there is nothing new to do.

Millions of dollars are spent each year in a search for life on other planets, any extra-terrestrial form of life. But really what are they expecting to find? It's just some desperate attempts to escape the routine. Earth or Mars, this galaxy or a galaxy far, far away! Humans or aliens with green or blue skin! Believe me it does not matter, you're only going to find the same routine. Aliens, eating, sleeping, reproducing and then fighting! Then they wonder -if they are smart enough- why is this boring universal routine?

If your answer for why we human keep on living? Is that we do it for the joy we find in living. Well, here I am, I have lost the charm of this routine! But I am still living, I want something! Yes, what keeps me alive seems to be the need for answers, I want to know why.

For if there were no answers to these questions, is there any meaning in staying alive?

The fact that I am able to ponder these questions makes me doubt that the answers are missing.

And if we have evolved to survive and have maximum pleasure, then evolving the ability to ask such existential questions would contradict the materialistic evolution. Now that we ask, we easily can end our existence for the lack of meaning, again, aren't we revolting against the laws of nature? Or was the ability to ask such existential questions the pinnacle of our evolution, or the reason of our creation?

Let us take a look at what we consider as humanity's great achievements, what make us unique and set us apart from the other forms of life on this planet, what affect our daily actions, our beliefs even our dreams:

Civilization.
Natural sciences.
And the metaphysical element 'spirituality'.

All are linked to our intellectual capacity in reacting to each other, the universe around us, and what's beyond!

About Civilization

Indeed we can argue that other organisms have some form of civilization. Maybe it's more evident in some insects such as ants and bees, in crows, whales and chimpanzees. These non-human civilizations might have many similar characteristics with human civilizations, such as: complex societies, social stratification, specialization of labor, a systems of communication and knowledge transfer, and some domination over the natural environment. Still, as humans we believe that we have achieved a higher level of complexity that sets us apart from these natural civilizations. I strongly doubt that any other known organism on planet Earth has the same intellectual level as us, our dominance is clear, regardless of how good or bad it is for us or the environment.

Henceforth, I will use the term civilization to refer to our advanced complex human socio-cultural system.

There is no need to list the similarities between ancient and current civilizations. It is enough to highlight some contents of the cuneiform tablets, the oldest writing system -so far, excluding pictograms, cave paintings and such- developed by the Sumerians in fourth millennium BC, in ancient Mesopotamia, the cradle of civilization as historians like to call it; the prices of fish, bread and sheep, receipts of delivery, a poem praising the warrior king, boasting about the might of his army and how they have burned and destroyed the cities of the enemy, a magical talisman to win the heart of a brave man or a beautiful woman, a simple law to punish the thief and the murderer. And a little contemplation about the stars in the sky…And when are we going to die?

Thousands of years have passed, we brag about having a better civilization now, how much do we humans love this word 'civilization', a term that gives us the illusion of being special or better, that we have control and that we understand the universe. We have evolved by many miles from that primitive cave man or those hunter gatherer societies.

Really! How?
We have countries, nations with flags and symbols, we have constitutions and laws, we have houses and palaces, we have libraries full of all kinds of books, we have factories, and we have super markets full of all our needs, Ooh! And we don't defecate in the jungle anymore (most of us at least!), we have toilet paper, we are just better.

No…no! We are better, we "gave" women the right to vote, to have education and to own propriety, and she can take of her clothes and walk naked, she has been "porn" a new! (But let's give her less money for her work!).

No…no! We are better, look at all these rockets and bombs, we can destroy the planet, we are the strongest, we are better.

But the polls and statistical analysis say we are better! Look at our stock markets, and all these colorful papers we print, all these machines, we are techno-better.

No… We are better, we live in forests and we protect the environment, we are eco-better.

Nah… Look at all these monuments and pile of rocks, our ancestors were the greatest, so we are historically better!

What about us! We worship a million deities, we must be better.

A million! We worship nothing (except ourselves!). Surly we are better.

Wrong! Look at my skin color, I am orange. (What!!!)

No…No… We are…
Well, SHUT UP!
You and you… and that orange clown over there.

Different names of the same reality. You all are living the same routine, food and drinks, clothes and sheep, reproduction and destruction, and a lot of addiction, on running away from the question.

A nation that repeats the routine more easily (for geographical climatic reasons for example!) and another nation aspires to acquire that which is in the hands of the other. They create a reason, an excuse to legitimize their forthcoming crime and aggression. How can we steal the land and resources without looking uncivilized after such primitive animalistic behavior (such arrogance!).

Look! Mmm... The other don't... Oh! The other is wearing a headgear! All these filthy headgears. And what about their long dresses, covering all the body! What an attack on human liberty! If we don't go and kill them now they will make us wear that! Let's go steal their land, their resources and their history!

"For the love of our civilization". Attaaaack!!!

The civilized aggressor simply forgot that the other is wearing that because they are living in the desert under the sun! Or because of their moral code! Availability of resources, etc. But come on who wants to think about that now! And after they steal the land and what's in it (stealing the routine!), many books will be written and many poets will write songs about the great, just war. How the force of good defeated the threat of those evil headgear wearing devils! (This seems absurd, but crazily enough some people have their intelligent reduced to this level).

Just look at what Rome had done to the image of all those who they stole their land and heritage! Many of which have much more advanced civilization and had a far richer history, like Carthage around most of the Mediterranean or the Celts in mainland Europe. Simply they have been stripped away from their humanity and they just called them "Barbaric", a bunch of uncivilized monsters! What a big lie it was (or it is). Spain did the same upon the conquest of the new world, and so did the United Kingdom there, as well in Africa and India! Or imperial Japan in China and the pacific, or imperial China with the Han vs barbarians under the Tianxia (All under Heaven) concept. To name a few, for many other -if not all- civilizations around the world did similar acts. Thanks to modern archaeologists and historians for revealing the greatness of many of these ancient "barbaric" civilizations.

But isn't that how states and empires are built?
A flag, a parrot and a sword.
And a LOT of blood.

And the most dangerous of them all is the parrot! For you should never believe all that is written in history books, nor what is offered to the masses in current mass media channels. Don't believe a bunch of delusional radicals who see conspiracy theories in everything! Nor believe a bunch of delusional ignorant that believe in the sainthood of the political systems. For the truth is not there nor there! Take a step away, distance yourself from the torrent of information and opinions, vary your sources and then contemplate. Really, contemplate a lot. Read about your "enemy" from their resources, read as a neutral observant and don't let emotions or any socio-historical prejudice cloud your logical thinking. And never let yourself be convinced that only by reading books you will reach ultimate truths. Sometimes books hurt more than they benefit! That is a famous writer, and that is an ancient book, and that is a genius of his time, he must say the truth!

For between the rocks is very little to gain
And between the lines is very little to learn
For some trees have a pleasant smell
Carrying many fruits but they will kill

.

Books can give you the impression that you are educated, and many "educated" people tend to stick firmly to the ideas in those first books they have read which gave them that impression of being educated. Indeed they have gained some knowledge, but the danger is in that feeling of satisfaction! The sense of satiation and repugnancy toward any new ideas. I know enough now and I don't need to know more! I already know the truth.

... Yeah, yeah! (I'm rolling my eyes)

This is pseudo-wisdom.

Unfortunately, many use civilization as an excuse to legitimize aggression, to look down upon the other. Civilization in this sense is just a tool to elevate any shameful morally wrong behavior on the individual micro-level, to a patriotic benevolent act at the society macro-level.

Some examples are torture, theft and population mass killing (genocide), where most of us agree on the negativity and immorality of these acts on the personal level (we will come back to that later), hence, these acts are punishable by laws all around the globe, and any individual who commit these "crimes" will be isolated or removed from the society. But, when the state which represent the summation of the individuals commit such atrocities, well! You know! They did it because it was necessary. Suddenly the guilt is removed, because you can't blame individuals, for if you ask them they will answer that they utterly disagree with theft or genocides. But they know that if the state does it, well the state is just an idea, you can't jail the state! Or order it to be executed! Except for few officials who might be so easily sacrificed as scapegoats, if things goes wrong with some other nations.

A recent example is NAZI Germany during the Second World War, where all the evilness was personified in Adolf Hitler and his party (leadership only not every member though!), while the masses stayed high above scrutiny. The same goes for the allied forces on the other side of the conflict, all the atrocities and systematic mass rape they did in Germany was just normal!
Oh, I forgot, they were fighting the devil!

We saw a similar scheme repeating in the Iraq war, where Bush and few of his administration members were blamed for lying regarding the presence of weapons of mass destruction in Iraq (as if the US doesn't possess it!), which lead to the military action against many innocent civilians in Iraq, leaving the American masses above questioning.

Now, I am not saying that we should criminalize all the population of certain countries, for indeed many were against such evil acts of war. And many have paid the cost of the foolishness of their leaders with the blood of their young children. But we should make a clear distinction and proper judgment on where does the responsibility lies; between the personal moral code and its reflection on the state, and between the moral code of the state and its reflection on each individual.

If you want another proof of our wrong conception of civilization, just look at our heroes...

Soldiers, knights and warrior kings, those who killed the most! Those who have beaten the enemy and crushed the other. We revere them, we place them above us, we make them legends, we place paintings and statues of them in every corner and we write poems about them and fill our history books with fantasies about their divinity.

It seems that I have a very negative opinion about civilization. Well let me clarify then...

I am definitely not against civilization and I don't think or claim that civilization is evil. On the contrary and as I said before, human civilization sets us apart from other organisms here on Earth, and it has a strong influence on our behavior on the larger social level, as well on the individual level. I am just against the misuse of the term or the idea, especially when it is reduced to mean statehood, nationalism, tribalism or worst as in racial supremacy. And based on these misconceptions of the term many atrocities have been and will be committed in the name of civilization.

An example of this misuse is what happened during the "colonization" (exploitation!) of Africa by some imperial European states in the past three centuries. For if the European regimes (and many -not all- citizens) <u>of that time</u> understood civilization justly, where civilization is a mechanism to learn and evolve away from primitive materialistic animalistic automatic behavior, to a more morally and intellectually superior behavior, based on reason, experience and a metaphysical moral reference -more on that later- for the sake of happiness and peace of all the human race and the planet. They would not have inflected the damage and injustice upon millions of their brothers in humanity in Africa, and instead of slavery and state sponsored resources theft (of those who have slightly got delayed in their technological advancement), it would have been more beneficial and morally correct to have helped them to advance, to develop and exploit their potential for the best of all humanity, to collaborate rather than to dominate. Now that would have been truly civilized.

Civilization is essential for our existence, for our prosperity and for our humanity. For chaos and anarchy is not a viable option, since in the absence of regulations, laws and morality, we cannot coexist in cities of millions of inhabitants, or have scientific and technological advances.

This was a showcase of the routine on the larger scale; the society level. But what about the smaller scale, the Family.

About Family

Another escape route from answering!
An attempt to break the routine!

Everything is harder when I am alone, why not seek some help?

I am skipping the biological evolutionary aspect of the family, simply because you can opt-out from having a family. Thus, you can negate this biological drive and this makes it optional at least for us humans, where another type of need might be the drive behind establishing a family.

A search for another human who might help me find the -or a- meaning, let's break the routine or at least ignore it. A wife a husband, or a friend.

Now I am busy by what he or she is doing. The cure seems to work, but wait a minute!

He is also asking and wondering, now both of us have questions, how did we overlook that? Let's block that, let's fill the void then...

Children!

One, two...maybe ten or more, it doesn't matter let's keep making babies until the void is filled.

I am much better now, there is a meaning to my life, I am a father or a mother, and I sacrifice for my children.

I am busy now, I have no time for questions. Don't talk to me now, I do it all for the sake of my children.

I start with a big sincere thanks for all parents, for their effort and patience, for their sacrifice and unconditional love.

But!
Let's put the emotions aside and let's talk logic.
Where is the achievement here?

Reproduction is not that special, every living thing has the capacity to reproduce (with some exceptions), from viruses to bugs to cats. You just do what billions of other organisms do, nothing new here.

Aren't you just another slave for the instinct, just like them? Why so proud then? We are not even the best in it! For the weakest fish lays millions of eggs, and some elephant families have more love and sincere bonds than many human families do.

Ooh! Maybe you have forgotten then!
Or do you pretend to have forgotten?

You are not running away from questions by taking a family, for it's not the goal of your life. It's just another dose of drug that help give you the sense of importance and safety, it makes it easier to have the delusion of superiority and purpose, another ego satiation act.

Suddenly having a family and children does not look that altruistic! Let me be clear here…

I am not against having a family and children, as I said, it's a noble and benevolent act, if you are not a moral nihilist or purely self-centered individual. By which I mean you realize that the partner and children are separate equal individuals and not an extension to your power or a mean to extend your presence after your death. So if having children and family makes you happy then by all means do it, for it is very rare to find things that bring true joy these days.

But! Please don't be overly conceited, vanity is not justified here, like you did something special that no one else have done before! It's an earthly routine.

And most importantly, don't let it stop you from the search for the true meaning of your existence.

Ask…
All the questions…
ALL…
Especially "why?".

Many Philosophies and One Reality

You or I, will never claim that we were the first or the only individuals who thought about the meaning behind every action or the meaning behind existence itself. Surely I am not the only one who choose to keep on living in search for the answers, for how many great minds have went that bath before, many are famous and others are unknown. The list is so long to be mentioned here, each philosopher belonged to a different school, which had its different terms and classifications of philosophical topics. But as we shall see, all philosophies known to humans belong to two categories only, or we can say all are part of one duality.

As wisdom seekers, there is a unity in our state and in our question, but how many of us have got the answer and how many have reached the truth? And if any have ever reached it, what was it?

Oh! A moment of happiness, I see 'what' and 'how' here, these are easier to answer. For we can simply go back to the writings of those inquisitive minds who lived or are still living among us, then analyze their methods and conclusions that produced philosophies and hypotheses that answered all these human intellectual inquiries.

Of course I am not going to go through each and every philosophy in detail, for that will need hundreds if not thousands of pages. But we can discuss the main primary logical paradigm that underlie these seemingly different philosophies, as I mentioned; the philosophical reasoning duality.

For the clever can fathom the simplest gesture.

So we start with these philosophies that avoided answering the absolute holistic ultimate 'why', or simply reached a conclusion that there is no why, no telos nor any meaning.

Materialistic Philosophies

These philosophies tend to focus mainly on the human activities (the routine), and try to analyze it, then organize it, from the theoretical idealist level to the individual level and finally to the global (societal) level. These philosophies compete in presenting the best answers for the primitive why, but usually ignore or fall short of answering the absolute holistic ultimate why.

But why is that?

Materialistic philosophies critical thinking -usually!- is based on one fundamental core conjecture: where the universe / nature / matter / energy is the reference, or the ultimate source beyond causality. Or as Spinoza have put it "Deus, sive Natura" nature or God, whether it's an active or passive presence.

While the place of humanity usually is viewed in two ways:

1) Humanity is a results of nature, just another meaningless accident of the physical laws. Thus, humans have no special place nor superiority, and any action or thought we have can be explained based on these physical laws. Again, nature is the reference.

2) Humanity is the ultimate result of the materialistic evolution, we are the center of the universe (now!), and even reality itself is shaped by our mental perception. Or at least we evolved to have sufficient understanding to exert control over the physical realm. Thus, humans are the reference, in other words; humans are Gods.

With a brief contemplation, we notice the similarity in reasoning in these views. The reference is always an innate self-reference, nature is the reference of itself, or humans are the reference of themselves. The only difference is that taking nature as the reference is far more reasonable, because in the end humanity is indeed a product of this nature and there is nothing more to us than what physics can't explain (well, they believe so!).

Also it's worth mentioning that they all agree on the absence or the redundancy of any metaphysical aspects such as God or soul.

To be clear, I am not judging this reasoning whether it is right or wrong, I am merely mentioning it as an activity that have been done by humanity.

Some famous examples of these materialistic philosophies are: Capitalism, Communism, Fascism, Natural Sciences, Epicureanism, Hegelianism, Nihilism, Humanism and Postmodernism.

All of which took the human (supreme leader/state) as the reference of reasoning. Except the natural sciences, postmodernism and nihilism, where nature was the reference, and humanity was reduced to another insignificant meaningless accident.

As for ethics, strangely some have derived it from these meaningless natural accidents! Others simply based it on some personal materialistic gain. For example in epicureanism anything that maximize your happiness is good, while in capitalism all that maximize capital and your ability to consume is good, and in communism all that come from the proletariat is good, and finally in fascism all that the party/state decide is good.

While the brave nihilists and postmodernists clearly declared that there is no good nor evil, or as Aleister Crowley have put it in the book of the law (Liber AL vel Legis): "Do what thou wilt", or his other aphorism which fit the natural sciences view on the source of morality "he who knows the HOW does not care about the WHY". Even though he was not a materialistic philosopher by definition (more on that later).

Now, the most reasonable and straightforward conclusion came from Nietzsche, when he declared that "God is dead", so he argued that by pulling away the religious belief and God as a reference, the morality that was derived from that system also goes away. This morality is by no means self-evident, in other words morality can't be derived from mathematical equations.

That is to say, in a materialistic philosophy that omits God from the equation, there is no justification for morality. Thus the true atheist must be a moral nihilist, with no God you are the God, you make your own laws and all the world revolves around you. Without God it's not wrong to kill, steal, abuse and exploit, all for personal gain. There is no obligation of being nice, compassionate, altruistic, honest, agreeable, humble, etc. with other people, unless it benefits you, no higher morality here.

Now atheists generally are not "mean" due to a number of reasons among which are cowardice and the practicality in being part of the society, but mainly, they don't break the moral code because they are not true atheists. That is to say, there are some residual remnants of the religious beliefs in their psyche, implemented and amplified by living in a society, where hierarchy is established beyond any hope or means of deconstructing it, and at the top of the pyramid there will always be the "God" figure, which transcend the hierarchy itself and determine the right and wrong (the source of the moral code).

The moment that an atheists adhere to a moral code, they are consciously or subconsciously basing this on dogmas rather than reason, they are being pseudo-atheists, who killed "God", then erected the carcass as an idol!

Again, I am not judging whether this is good or bad, I am merely stating the logic behind such philosophies.

Coming back to materialistic philosophies. There are few thing we have to consider when we analyze the rationale behind these different perspectives of reality, morality and society.

For example, the historical atmosphere where many of these thinkers have shaped their ideas in response to the socio-political situation they lived in. Some were dreamy and ideal, some were nationally motivated, some others meant to fight against some established tyrannical institutes (monarchy and church), some were fascinated or perplexed by the new scientific discoveries and the new technological advances, and finally, others merely had some personal interests (sense of responsibility, compassion, etc.).

So we have to be careful when analyzing or accepting any philosophy, and the socio-historical even personal contexts should be taken into account. Otherwise we will end up with a self-inflicted prejudice, misunderstanding, false pithiness or false amplification, or even it could reach a degree of sanctification of these philosophies.

To come back to the main topic, which of those philosophies gave a true answer to the absolute holistic ultimate why?

When humans were Gods, the answers came varied according to the needs, materialistic gain and socio-political atmosphere. Where some argued that the answer was achieving equality and prosperity for each and every individual, guaranteed by the state or the sufficiently scientific (rational) developed society (by force!). While some others were braver and without shedding away from the materialistic underlying principle, advocated that the survival of the fittest -or the strongest- in a wild cold Darwinian jungle, was the only meaning that is there.

Meh!

To be honest, I don't care that much! For the results were almost always similar, some fascistic and other failure-istic states (you can review the last 400 years of our history).

All arguing about the same routine, without a solid universally accepted reference for morality, they even simply did some plagiarism with cosmetic modification of other metaphysical philosophies (religions), which have resulted in the transfer of the sanctification of God to sanctification of the state, the party, the nationality or the individual (self-sanctification), except that the later has no meaning to it.

Or they have resulted in the desanctification of everything, including humanity itself, resulting in a system that consider people as mere resources or tools that can be exploited, exactly as all other things in nature. That resulted in a systematic destruction of the environment, the society and even the individual.

Sorry, but I'm not a tool nor an obedient patriot citizen, I refuse to adhere to moral codes without justifications, I am not limited and I refuse to be rationalized into schemes and paradigms of the elite ruling class and their technocrats. I am not a number, in fact none of us is a number, each is a unique individual, so don't just refer to us as statistics!

I am aware that there are some positive aspects to some of the materialistic philosophies, like some advances in science and technology, but on the moral and psychological level, we have to admit that they have a big problem. Like we are heading to one of the dystopian scenarios in the comics of the brilliant Alejandro Jodorowsky. War, famine, inequality, corruption, mass depression, racism, pollution and many other problems persist even increased, and the promised earthly paradise was never realized. People were forced to chase some variations of the American dream, where our needs even our dreams are predetermined, and we are stuck in a limited self-centric routine, empty from true meaning, we just do it because it's efficient! Socially acceptable! Pragmatic! And a potent drug, the real "das opium des volkes"!

On the other hand, when nature was God, the materialistic philosophy answer to this question was: there is no meaning to the why, nor any other question, it's all relative and quite pointless mental endeavor. The whole universe and what's in it is just an accident, and every action is a result of a random chance, no point to any of our human actions, simply there is no teleological explanation to any of this. It is just "is".

But is it really? Just "is"!

I certainly don't know how those got that level of confidence to make such claims?

But if someone really believe in this explanation, all I can say then is: live as the famous quote from the sportswear company Nike put it "Just do it." What a perfect motto that fits the materialistic philosophies.

If you truly believe that there is no answers, and think that our existence is meaningless, then you are free to "just do it". Keep repeating the routine without the philosophical pondering. Be another cog in a meaningless revolving cosmic machine.

Try to enjoy your spinning!
I guess…

Go! Be automatic, be another slave for the blind nature, and ignore your ability to think beyond nature!

But please remember that others have the right to doubt your belief in this blind chance and randomness. No matter how much that sounds logical in your head: That nothing really has a meaning, all came by accident, a result of blind nature. Yet somehow, me the self-conscious and rational being, accept to be a slave to this irrational randomness, suffering each day with another 8 billion similar copies, competing on space and resources, on false control and dominance over nothing!

To live!
That "is" all!

Just spinning and is-ing!

Then we die!
…Damn!

Sorry, but I will not accept this bacterial life (I'm not committing suicide, relax!). Not accepting it not because of arrogance or some egocentric pride. Nor because I am fighting the reality to give myself some purpose or false motivation to keep on living.

My ability to ask these existential questions -questions that transcends the materialistic universe- makes me doubt.

So does beauty…

Beauty!

I will confess...

From my aforementioned description of the universal routine we live in, it seems that I hate all that is there in the universe!

No! Without a doubt it's a routine, and even if you sensed some negativity in my description, I must remind you that I am not judging the act for itself, the negativity in my opinion is in doing any action without thinking about its meaning. Then, it is just stupidity.

Now that this point is clear...

There is beauty, even in this universal routine.

That sensation when you listen to classical music, as if that who composed it have found some divine secrets. It fills you with happiness, joy, satisfaction, peace and love, then it transcends you above the materialistic world.

No matter how much I write, I can never describe the sensation of beauty. That beauty in everything, in music, in a painting of an artist, in the human form, in flowers, in colors, fragrance and shapes, in the scenery of a forest filled with mist, or prairies covered with snow, there is beauty in everything.

Mmm, but can't we explain beauty in materialistic terms too (or only!). You are attracted to what brings you materialistic gain or benefit. So you can survive and compete in this wilderness we call universe.

Really?!
For example, what is the materialistic explanation for loving Beethoven's fifth symphony?

Maybe I can answer that. It fills a void! Simply when you listen to a tone, it occupy your thinking, it might activate a part of your brain where it might bring back a memory. Or maybe the secret is in the musical pattern itself, a simple repetition that is easy to recognize and memorize, which makes it familiar, and 'familiar' is safe and comfortable.

Same for beauty in the human body, it's for protection and survival, also for reproduction. You choose the strongest and more physically healthy individual, no real beauty here, just materialistic gain.

Maybe! But you and I know very well that our sense of beauty is much more than these simple explanations. For example, why we see beauty in a mathematical equation! in calligraphy? In the shape of a building! Or in the stars in the sky! As I said, there is beauty in everything, and in many instances I can't find any materialistic explanation for it.

Sensation of beauty!

Sensation!

Isn't it just a response to some stimuli by our nervous system? But then it transform to emotion, but what are emotions? For falling in love with the beauty of a musical piece, or a natural scenery is much more than a series of chemical signals traveling along our neurons, nor it is an innate property of the frequency of light and sound itself. For there is a difference between the cause and the effect.

For example, we don't say the computer is intelligent when it solves a mathematical equation, but we say it's an effect of an intelligent programmer, who is the cause or the source of intelligence. Same goes for love, the love for your parents, partner or children, even the love for music, nature or an equation, is not the chemical signal -reduced to oxytocin- that accompany the sensation, that, is merely the effect of some higher cause. For surely you too agree that each love emotion is different in away from the other. Chemical signals are tools that links the body to the self-consciousness (the soul!).

Soul!
What is a soul?
Is it the ego? The "I" and "you"?

The causative source that has the power behind the control panel (the brain)!

Maybe it is what is ordering my hand to rise up now! For no specific materialistic gain, not for food nor for defense, not even for pleasure! I just raise it because I want to raise it, challenging the law of gravity and that of conservation of energy for what is beneficial to me! And if I didn't want to raise it, there was no physical power that could've done it! So is the soul or the spirit this causative force that transcend the physical universe?

Doesn't that reduce the brain to a very complicated keyboard? For if you press the letter "O" followed by the letter "H" the word "OH" will appear on the screen. You the intelligent source have caused it to appear, you perceived it as a "word", and only you can give it a meaning.

OH!

Aren't all those brain activities we see in brain activity scans are merely keys being stroked to transfer the data from the material plane to the consciousness plane? And when some part of this input machinery has a failure in function, some of these communications are compromised, exactly as what will happen when controlling a computer or a machine.

Wait a minute!

What soul or spirit you are talking about!
I only believe what I see (or sense).
I only believe in empirical science.

Well there is a problem in adopting a mechanistic materialistic explanation of human or let's say animalistic behavior and many other psychological phenomena.

For example, how can some similar chemical reactions result in different meaning perception like smell, vision, taste, love, euphoria, etc. Let alone the more complicated questions such as the free well and self-consciousness.

This mind–body problem is as old as philosophy itself. You can read more about it in the writings of ancient Greek philosophers and later in the writing of Descartes who defended the Cartesian dualism, where the mental can exist outside the corporal, and the corporal itself cannot think. Some simply refute the notion of any metaphysical soul when explaining any intellectual psychological phenomena, while others argue that there should be a scientific method that takes soul into account when studying these psychological phenomena. One example is the book 'The Soul Hypothesis' by Mark C. Baker and Stewart Goetz.

Maybe It's worth trying at least!
Isn't that what science is all about!

But, what is science all about?

The Church of Natural Sciences

No! I'm not talking about the cult of reason and their temple of reason (Temple de la Raison) during the French revolution. Breaching a new religion using the mantra "Liberté, égalité, fraternité". I am talking about natural sciences as of now, and as a philosophical (epistemological) method.

Now, as a scientist, a member of this well-established universal scientific "community", I will tell you something that strangely many of us prefer not to emphasize for the commoners (the non-specialized scientists); we observe, we doubt, then we build rational conjectures (smart guessing), then finally we believe.

Let me give you an example:

Ancient astronomers knew that the earth is a sphere or a globe, many believed that Earth was the center of the universe and all the stars and planets revolves around it. Well, based on their capacities at that time, this was the smartest guess they could have come up with, according to their observations, everything seemed to revolve around Earth.

Fortunately, the beauty of the scientific method is the ability to empirically test any hypothesis. With the development of many new tools and more advanced mathematics, and the accumulation of observations from Babylon to Egypt to Athens, to India and China. To the great improvements in the scientific method in the golden age of Islam, followed shortly by the renaissance in Europe. The geocentric theory was falsified, as it failed to explain many of the observation, and it didn't represent the reality.

Thus, many scientist adopted heliocentrism, where earth and all the other planets revolves around the sun. A note worth mentioning here: heliocentrism was known in ancient times as well, it has been only rediscovered, for the first model of it was developed by Aristarchus of Samos in the 3rd century BC. What Ibn al-Shatir 14th century and later Copernicus 16th century have done, was the correction of the Ptolemaic models of the Sun, Moon and planets, which lead us to the rediscovery that we go around the sun not the other way around.

Indeed this was an important rediscovery, for its philosophical implications on the place of humanity in the universe, and it's frank contradiction of the adopted narrative by the church at that time.

But, what really matter here is not the reaction of the ancient scientists, but that of the commoners. The non-specialized majority, the baker, the farmer, the soldier and the blacksmith. Yesterday the earth was the center, today it's the sun!

I'm sure most of them were not able nor qualified to go into an in depth scientific or philosophical debate. They just had to trust the words of the scientists, to trust their honesty and abilities to make rational conclusions at least in their specialties. But in that moment, there was some scientists who advocated geocentrism while others advocated heliocentrism, so whom they should've believed?

From antiquity until this day, people believe the majority, more precisely what we call the scientific consensus.

To be clear…

I am not against the scientific method, I don't advocate marginalizing it nor abandoning it. That will be utterly stupid.

The scientific method is one of humanity's greatest achievements. I just wanted to highlight the term "scientific consensus", for in all natural sciences when we say facts we usually mean: the most logical explanation that describe observations and tangible reality, this explanation is supported by the majority of specialized scientists, but! There is always some space for doubt and to challenge that consensus, when this consensus fail to explain or contradicts any new observations (measurements). So, we go back and adjust or formulate new theories that fits and explain the new data (another smart guessing).

One good example is the standard model in physics, a combination of theories distilled into some beautiful mathematical equations that explain most of the physical phenomena in our universe. What is matter and what is energy, how they exchange from one form to another, how elements came to be, when a star was born and when it might die, and what exactly was that cute heart shape on the planet Pluto? (A planet! Don't' you mean a dwarf planet? Again with the consensus, I don't know but last time I checked we still call a dwarf human a human!).

With all the greatness of this standard model, still! It fails to explain every single physical phenomena. For example, the dark matter and dark energy. Where no consensus has been reached on their existence nor their essence. Another example can be found in the quantum world, such as the quantum entanglement, where some particles appear to be linked across great distances and can exchange information instantly, with zero time!

In conclusion, we do not reach the 100% absolute certainty. The best we have is a theory that has a very, very high chance of being true in explaining reality.

Very, very high! You might ask, but how much is that? 60%, 90%, or is it 99.99999% certainty?

Here I can justify the use of the term "the church of natural sciences". For as bishops gather in a church to determine whether Jesus Christ is a man or a God, and some others try to conceal the schism by advocating that he is both! The majority, whether it is a majority by number, political or military power, reach a consensus, and they determine what is true and what is not! (Of course it was what suited the Roman emperor most, referring to First Council of Nicaea 325 AD).

We as a scientific society behave in a similar way to bishops, we decide the rules of the game. In one discipline of science, the scientific bishops decide that 55% is a majority, but aren't they being too lenient! Well, in some disciplines of science it is hard if not impossible to reach higher level of confidence. Thus, those scientific bishops lower the bar so they can maintain a research career by publishing papers! But in some other disciplines of science -mainly physics- they usually accept 99.9...9% certainty to reach a consensus, now that is more convincing. But let me remind you, it is still not 100%, it is a very educated and smart guess, with a very, very high confidence level that we believe it is true. Again our belief might change in light of new measurements or inexplicable observations.

What really bothers me these days, is the way that science is presented to the masses. All the 99.99..% are presented as 100% unchangeable ultimate facts. Sometime due to our arrogance and pride in the scientific method, and sometimes scientists do it to show how much beautiful the scientific method is. This scientific breaching is very evident in TVs, newspapers, social networks and even in schools.

Unfortunately, most people out of their trust of the scientific community or due the lack of proper training in science or the well to argue, they believe the scientific bishops without much questioning.

See how it is much easier to sell a product or offer a medication just because it name has some fancy chemical formulas. A 100mg L-ascorbic acid is more convincing than a cup of orange juice.

So, when someone say I believe in science. He is correct to use "believe", for I also believe in what has been proven to a high degree of certainty by rigorous experiments -if possible- and what has withstand the different attempts of falsification, until that conjecture has reached a very high level of confidence to call it a fact. In the end, I am a scientific bishop, a baptized member according to the church of natural sciences.

But if scientific theories are prone to change, how can we rely on them to judge the ultimate right and wrong? And why we monopolize science as the sole method to reach the truth? Science is rarely applied to history for example, but most of us don't doubt that Julius Caesar have defeated the Gauls! And their king Vercingetorix was paraded through the streets of Rome and then executed by strangulation on Caesar's orders, the vast number of different people reporting an incident might suffice. Nor you need a scientific experiment to explain why you are in love with someone! On glance will suffice.

But most importantly, why we don't lose faith in the church of natural sciences when it adopt some false views about our fundamental understanding of the universe? And if some of its members commit a fraud or invented a nuclear bomb that can wipe us from the face of earth, we don't criminalize the whole institution and we don't declare it as the source of all evil!

AH!

Because there is a difference between a philosophy and the actions of individuals, even if those individuals were the majority. That's why we don't abandon nor criminalize the scientific method, no matter how wrong or corrupted some scientist are in certain places or eras. For how many fake research papers we have now, some do it for money, others for fame and others because of some political agendas.

Oh, how I wish that we don't have such hypocrisy and double standards.

The scientific method is a philosophy, like other philosophies. So don't judge the other philosophies differently. Don't criminalize it due to the actions of some individuals. Let your judgment be based on the abstract ideas, the logical, epistemological and ethical principles.

So, science is good!
Of course it is.
But, it's not enough.

Science is the best materialistic philosophy that answers many questions regarding our perceptible universe. Science excel in answering the "how" question, I am even encouraged to claim that it has almost a complete monopoly over that question. But science fails when attempting to answer the "why" question, for "why" is above the scope of science, since it transcends the materialistic plane, and that's why science fails.

For example, in physics we have a lot of universal constants, the speed of light in vacuum 299,792,458 km/s, Planck constant $6.626070040(81) \times 10^{-34}$ J·s, and many more other constants, for gravity, magnetism, etc. What are they, and "how" we derived them, is the domain of science. But, "why" they have such values? Or why they are there in the first place? Here science fails to give a solid answer. In best cases the answer will be it's an accident! Or maybe they are as this because of some higher physical laws that we don't know yet! But what are those laws then? And why they are there? Isn't that just an attempt to run away from the answer?

Some argue, if all these values are there by chance, then how unlikely it is for it to be just right to allow the universe to exist as it is now! Very fine tuned to allow subatomic particles to form, then atoms, then stars and planets, then earth and finally life itself. Well, many scientist will quickly answer it is very unlikely indeed, but the probability is not zero! A 0.000(Gazillion)001%, but not 0.

Or as the famous British mathematical physicist Roger Penrose have calculated once, for the probability of the initial entropy conditions of the Big Bang, that allowed for a highly orderly universe out of a highly entropic (chaotic) universe. The odds against such an occurrence were on the order of 10 to the power of 10^{123} to 1. It worth mentioning that the estimated number of atom in the universe is 10^{80}, and usually in probability theory, odds of less than 1 in 10^{50} equals "zero probability".

Well, what is the solution then if we want to keep our belief in chance or "ordo ab chaos"?

Aha! There is a solution, there must be an infinite number of universes then. Since infinity is infinitely large, the near zero probability become inevitably probable. Well, it's either this multiverse hypothesis, or we have to recognize that on the other side, the 99.99(Gazillion)99% is the anti-chaos, the probability of "ordo ab ordo", where the values have a teleological meaning, they are predetermined via an intelligent factor, an intelligent designer!

God!

I don't know since when we accept near zero as valid confidence level to build our belief on! Isn't that the reason why scientist and others always aim to find ways to increase our confidence level in a theory?

But isn't raising the confidence via the proposition of a multiverse hypothesis rather pointless? First if it is scientific then it must be empirical, not only idealistic. But for a moment, let's say we have already have proven the multiverse existence, the question persists, where do all these universes came from? Where do they exit in, for isn't the summation of all of them become "the universe"? What are the physical laws that govern them? And why these laws are there? We will simply face the same questions again.

Some scientists prefer to argue that science should not be used in such way in philosophical discourse. The extremely low probability of the universal constant to support life should not be a proof of an intelligent designer, on the contrary, it's a proof of a poorly designed universe! Well, what a strange logic is that! For if life is that hard to kick start and maintain in this harsh universe, then this make the interference of an intelligent designer more necessary and crucial. And if you want to keep science away from any theological discourse, then don't use it to disprove God too. But I find that very illogical, for science is a philosophy too.

Speaking of belief and probability, usually in life we don't wait for the 100% confidence to make our decisions. Let's say you are in a ship that is about to sink, the captain tells you: you have 0% chance of survival if you stay on the ship, but you have 1% chance of survival if you jump into water now and try to swim to safety! You in a hurry answer: Ok, I'll jump now, 10% is much better than 0%. The captain then adds: but wait a minute, you have 90% chance of survival if you come with me to the lifeboat. Now suddenly the 10% is too little of a confidence level compared to the 90%. A sane individual will definitely choose the lifeboat option. Plus, the advice is coming from the captain, he knows what he is talking about. He is more qualified than the passengers to make that educated conjecture. So if you choose the 90% over the 10%, you will defiantly never go for the 0.001% or less! Now, I can't fathom how can someone risk it all for a near zero chance?

Again, just asking.

Anyhow, remember, I am not trying to convince you with

any certain point of view, I am simply putting forward what is the logic of each side, the <u>believers</u> in chance and the "believers" in order.

What matter is, in the end, regardless of what side you choose to consider more logical. You will have to believe in a starting point that defy explanation, and -forever!- beyond our intellectual capabilities.

If you follow the materialistic path, then this point of origin will be nature, the "uncreated" matter or energy. The talk about matter and energy popping out of vacuum is ridiculous, what nothingness they are talking about? The "vacuum" is full of energy fields already!

On the other hand, if you decide that the probabilities in the materialistic explanation are unacceptable, then you must believe in an intelligent designer (a non-materialistic source) as the point of origin.

Well, whether it's this or that, both will end up being a belief. One has an extremely low probability of being true and -by the definition of this or that- the other has an extremely high probability of being true.

But I only believe in what I see, measure and experiment.

Well, Then how many white circles I placed in this book pages?

What?!

Yeah, maybe you have noticed in the past pages some black circles that intersect or contained some white circles. For I have placed seven white circles in this book.

If you only believe in what you can experiment, go count them now, I'll wait…

.

..

…

They are five, maybe!
But where are the other two circles?

I swear that I have placed them, but you can never detect them unless you have the original electronic copy that I am typing now.

So you have to trust my word now.
Or don't!
It doesn't matter, for this will not change the truth.

Yes, you believing or disbelieving in their existence will not change the fact that they are truly there. Not all things in the universe are tangible or let's say detectable or perceivable, but your inability to conceive them does not change the fact that they are truly exciting. For our sensory capacity has limits, no matter how advanced our measurement tools are.

For the truth itself cannot be veiled, but it's you who are veiled from perceiving it.

They are seven.

Again and to be clear, I don't in any way advocate abandoning the scientific method. I am merely stressing on realizing its limits, and to highlight the doubt in what we usually label as ultimate facts, unchangeable and unquestionable. For today's norms could become tomorrow's mistakes. I also advocate using the scientific method to derive the most logical answers, the one with the highest probability of explaining observations.

This empirical method can be extended to other philosophical theories too.

Well, then how we answer the "why" question?
If not by natural sciences, then how?
…

Don't worry, there will be no need for costume parties, nor any occult rituals during secret meetings to call upon the ancient wisdom. Again, the truth cannot be concealed and it's not exclusive to anyone.

All you need is some logic and critical thinking away from emotions and hopes.

Metaphysical Philosophies

They are as plentiful as summer harvest. Some of them are clear and simple, other are overly complicated, as if they go in a labyrinth again and again only to end at the starting point each time. Some are full of answers, other are empty. Some are ancient, other are modern, some are personal other are collective, some are popular while other are secretive.

Of course, it's beyond the scope -or the need- of this book to discuss each and every one of them in details. Again we can simply discuss the underlying principles that generated and shaped these philosophies.

A human observing the environment. Noticing patterns in nature and in the actions of the living (the universal routine). The human then question the meanings behind all of these actions, then the meaning of existence. Then a philosophy is born.

For example, Buddha has forsaken the life of luxury as a prince, the moment he realized that all he has will go away at some point. Then he took on a journey to find the meaning of life, in hope to find an answer for the meaning behind the universal routine. Or maybe a way to change it! Or stop it! And after many attempts of prolonged fasting -which almost killed him- and at the age of 35 he declared that he have reached "the" answer; he became aware or enlightened (a Buddha).

The answer he reached was that you have to escape this routine, this cycle of birth and rebirth or reincarnation or samsara, to reach the nirvana or moksha, the freedom from the samsara in Indian religions. Only then you are liberated from these reincarnation cycles, you are free from the materialistic desires and of 'willing' itself. You are literally 'blown out', you lose yourself and you merge or go back to the spirit of the universe. Mmm…

To be blown out! To lose myself! To lose my will! But by doing this, am I not escaping from the answers? Just answering "why" with I will stop asking "why".

My answer to Buddhism is: I don't hate anyone and I am not blinded by materialistic animalistic desires, I guess my description of the universal routine was clear. But I don't want to lose my will, I don't want to lose myself, I want to stay "me" the conscious free intelligent being, I'll never wish for a complete dissolution of my ego, into an unconscious component that will lose the ability to question and seek answers.

Sorry, I don't think this satisfactory answer. It could be comfortable for some (or many!). But I see it as an attempt to escape from answers. Another drug! To quench our inability to answer the 'why', and justify nihilism.

To be clear, I don't discuss the ethical aspects -as in moral codes of societies- of any metaphysical philosophy here. I only analyze their ability to provide logical answers to existential questions.

I don't know exactly how Mr. Siddhartha Gautama (Buddha) has lived his next 45 years of his life. But it seems he lived the same routine that we always had, and his hope was to be blown out forever. Makes me wonder why didn't he blew himself out at the age of 35 already! How the unconscious universal spirit was going to judge him? Or was it conscious? Oh, but he is part of it, so it will judge itself! Then punish itself! Then banish itself! Why all these emanations and rejoining cycles? Is there a meaning to it? Since all is one and one is all, we will always end up where we have started! This seems rather to be a pointless mechanical glitch. No true justifications for individual morality nor suffering, nor any true answers for why all that cyclic mechanism is there in the first place! Also, why all this idol adoration! I thought Buddha has lost himself in the soul of the universe, who are we praying for then? And why do we need a statue? Again, it is just natural to ask.

Since we have started in the east, most of the metaphysical philosophies there are derived from Buddhism, Hinduism, Shamanism or Animism. In short terms, the worship of nature. For all agree that there is a universal spirit, which has emanated all the other spirits, it is a living force, but it seems rather unconscious primitive attractive force. That fills all the material plane and beyond, summarized in the mantra "all is one and one is all". But isn't that a materialistic philosophy then? We ended up worshipping nature, this time under some pseudo-spiritual assumptions, that nature has a spirit!

This also apply for what is known as the 'New Age', the European version of eastern (mainly Hindu) and some Native American shamanic religions. Which is in turn the child of the many spiritual movements at the end of the 19th century, such as the prominent Theosophical Society founded by Helena Blavatsky. Thelema founded by Aleister Crowley. And the older Freemasonry and its different flavors and branches. Many of which are closed clubs, claiming to have the absolute holistic ultimate truth, that was lost through eons, only to be maintained by a small group who operated secretly and hid all that knowledge by "magickal" occult symbolism, only to be revealed for the selected few!

I simply answer, there is no monopoly of the universal truth.

These spiritual philosophies give rather few morally acceptable -not totally justified- explanation for the universal routine in the form of harmony and respect to all the living things. For example, even when you kill and eat an animal, you kind of transferring or borrowing its vital force, it is not truly dead, since it is part of you now! All these seem to be comfortable answers justifying the universal routine, but these philosophies lack a solid explanation for the ultimate existential questions, the "whys". Usually they end up with; we will join the source again, and we will become gods, or merge into God!

One minute please!
I don't want to enter a religious debate that might stimulate the emotions or any prior socio-cultural indoctrination people might have.

So, briefly about metaphysical philosophies:
One origin with multiple interpretations.
Same story regardless of the names, one truth and

multiple examples. Attempts to explain universal or natural phenomena on the superficial and the occult level, to derive or discover a/the meanings.

Humans noticed the patterns in nature, repeating as if they are following universal laws. Every day the sun rises in the morning, then it sets at the evening. The moon has phases that repeat every month. There are four seasons in the year, the sun dies in winter and then resurrected in spring.

With some simplification, as if you are explaining something to a child, the ancient philosophers attempted to explain these natural phenomena to the masses. They found it was far easier to personify these phenomena as humans or other beastly forms, rather than discussing the abstract ideas. You can think of it as an old time entertainment activity, some superhero stories, philosophy was presented as modern-day comics. What you told the children in societies -these fantastical imagery- have turned to realities.

So the day and night became two men fighting, one win in the morning hours, then the other prevail when the sun set, now you can call them whatever you want, like 'Horus and Seth' as the Egyptians did. The sign for the sun in ancient cultures was the sun cross ($\bigoplus$), as if it is a wheel of a chariot that crosses the sky every day, a strong benevolent life giving entity, when it dies in winter life on earth mourns its death, waiting its resurrection in spring to celebrate life again. The bull, wheat, women are all symbols of fecundity, form the Sumerian Inanna, the Phoenician goddess Astarte, to the Egyptian cow goddess Hat-Hor, the Greek Aphrodite, to the Norse goddess Freyja, and the list goes on and on. All were derived from one original source.

The human spirit, the conscious ego, the wise heavenly element, which fell down and was trapped in a materialistic container. Imprisoned and suffering, fighting the animalistic desires (food, sleep, sex, etc.). Activities that fills its time and keep it distracted from its true self, its origin, truth and telos. Only by death, it is liberated from this material sarcophagus (the body), to heaven again. It is the beautiful Persephone who was kidnaped by Pluto to the underworld, it is Mithra of the Iranians, and it is the Hellenic Bacchus or Dionysus who was eaten by the Titans (twelve of them in reference to the twelve zodiac signs and the belief in their effect on human life), after he was distracted by material world from his true self, they ate him all except his heart (the heavenly essence of the human spirit), then Zeus Killed them and from their flesh he created humans, so Bacchus lives in us.

The example repeats with variation of the narrative and names. On these principles many occult philosophies have been established, including alchemy, you die to be porn again, you transform yourself from a low materialistic impurities (lead) to heavenly pure spirit (gold), through intellectual and spiritual growth or wisdom (the philosopher's stone).

Each culture tells the same story, adapting and changing the narrative to suit their environment and needs. These personified ideas changed gradually to gods and goddesses, and the natural elements like oak trees, wheat, corn, the sun, the moon, the zodiacs, the bull, boar and fish, all woven into the narrative, then became rituals and rites (religious practices).

Reenacting the story, some sacrifice a bull, some decorate a tree, some celebrate the rebirth of the sun god in spring, and others give offerings to idols, or elevate an ancestor or a king to godhood, and many other examples. The aim here is to highlight the similarities and derivation between all these religions. Unfortunately, these practices are usually sanctified at the action level, while the moral or meaning behind them is forgotten.

But what was the meaning?

To know the primal source, the ultimate cause of all that there is. The ONE, the creator of the universe, the source of order, the one that gave humans this transcendental powers to be self-conscious, intelligent, free, able to seek wisdom, ask questions and contemplate the abstract ideas beyond the animalistic material drive.

Wait!
Before you judge…

Again, I am not trying to convince you with anything here, actually I don't care what you choose to believe in. I am only showcasing what we have come up with so far as humans to explain our existence.

Two options:

Either there is no meaning for anything, all are just blind chances (no matter how low was the probability!) as we mentioned before in the section on materialistic philosophies. So no God, no meaning for the question "why" or the answer. But very strangely humans are inquisitive by nature and always seek to find the cause behind everything, always seeking that point of origin. This human behavior is a fact.

Some might ask, why it is a fact?
Well, here you are answering yourself.

Or on the other hand, there is more to us than the sum of the atoms of our body, governed by mathematical equations (laws!). Thus, God is an evident necessity, and there is a reason why we can ask. And we should seek answers, and search for meanings behind our actions, our existence, and the existence of existence.

Now you are free to choose whatever you want.

All I can say, I hope that as intelligent beings we somehow chose the more logical option, following scientific methods as much as we can, believing only after a thorough examination and contemplation, away from emotions and prior socio-cultural norms. But most importantly, no matter what you choose to believe in, please don't hurt the other, nor attempt to force your choice on them. You were free so let the other be free.

And as societies, let's be fair and tolerant. Let's respect the individual freedom of choice.

But aren't there an imminent conflict in such heterogeneous societies? For some ideas might contradict each other, or even clash.

Again, the society can be like an oil lamp, no matter what oil you put in it, it takes it, then turn it into light. Let's take the good in each philosophy, and re-emanate it as a light that illuminate the existence.

The existence!
But what is existence?

Leaves of Existence

In quantum physics a particle can have a dual states. In line with the uncertainty principle that highlight the limit to the precision within which certain pairs of physical properties can be measured. In other words, you can measure one property very precisely on the cost of measuring the other.

For example let's take light, which is both a particle and a wave (or neither!). Or we can say: depending on the way we measure it, it can manifest as a particle as in electromagnetism, or it can manifest as a wave as in dispersion of light by prisms (white light to rainbow).

But why this example?

As there is a dual state in quantum physics, I am having a quantum state of emotions now. I am happy but sad, I am content and discontent!

But how can you be happy and sad at the same moment?

I was confused before too, but then I realized the answer. For a moment, it seems happiness and sadness are two opposite things, but if you contemplate a little you will realize that both are in fact a description of one emotion duality.

I'll explain:

If you were to represent the emotions on a line, it'll look like this:

Happiness	Apathy	Sadness

And so does many other ideas…

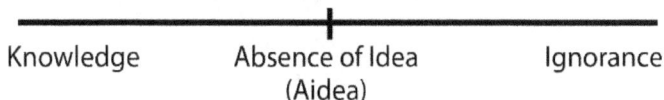

Knowledge	Absence of Idea (Aidea)	Ignorance

The list goes on and on…

Wow! We all know that.

Maybe! I just wanted to highlight that both of the opposite terms are in fact a description of the same line. And both are necessary for the line to exit.

This pairs of opposite ideas, or let's say duality is a universal phenomenon. Many philosophies have talked about it before, prominently Taoism as in the famous yin and yang, to Zoroastrianism to Islam. But wait! You said you have two states at the same time, I am not represented on this line, unless! Yes, let's bring the two ends together, to form a circle! No, to form a leaf shape.

The absolute idea of the feeling

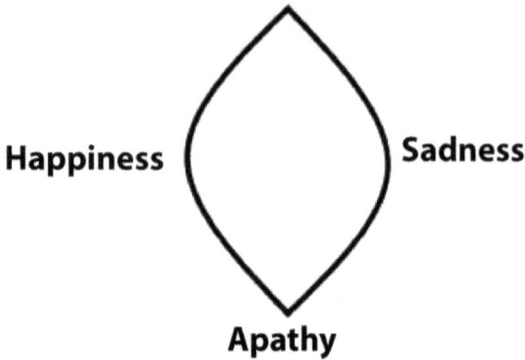

Happiness **Sadness**

Apathy

The absolute idea of change in extent

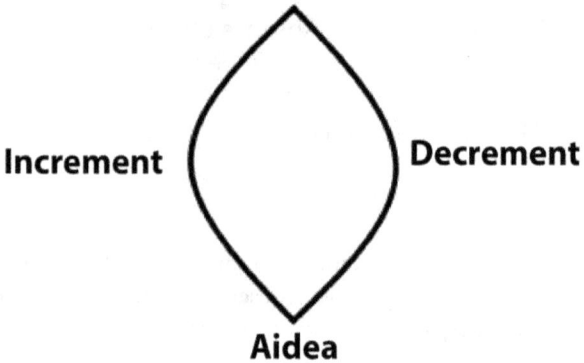

Increment **Decrement**

Aidea

But don't they cancel each other when they come together?

No... Both are there, in a quantum ideal state. They are only absent at the bottom of the leaf, where the idea disappear 'aidea', thus the 'a' suffix (without) 'idea'. Maybe a little math will make things easy!

The absolute idea (∞)

pair **pair**

Nothigness (0)

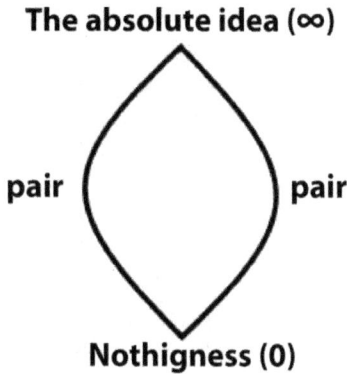

This duality in existence is a universal law. For everything there is an opposite thing that complement it and gives it a meaning. No meaning of darkness without light, no meaning for positivity without negativity and no meaning to happiness without sadness. Remove the pairs and the idea stop manifesting, the "quantum" ideal state is infinite (ideal) a metaphysical reality (the source), for it contains the opposites at an infinite original form. Once the idea manifests, the dual pairs are born in the objective plane.

To rephrase, the universe is this quantum ideal state manifested, a duality between infinity (ultimate ideas) and zero (nothingness). What we call universe, and all that in it from material/energy, actions, etc., all are ideas manifesting in pairs.

This talk about the ideal plane of existence seems Platonic, and the talk about the necessity of the pairs to exist in order for the ideas to manifest, seems Hegelian. And that might be true, but again I am emphasizing on both, the ideal is the infinite ultimate source of existents, what follow are mere manifestations of this ideal plane as dualities. You can think of it as a dream if you wish! Or as a computer simulation.

In your dream, your intelligence is the source of ideas, which manifest in the dream plane as dualities. You create a universe, full of beings, you give them characteristics and individualities. Now for those beings in the dream, they see themselves as a real existence, and indeed they are real in the dream plane. Same goes in our computer simulations, objects created in the simulations are real for themselves, there are laws that governs their behavior, and the universe around them. They might be intelligent entities, for example they could have an AI guiding their behavior, now the computer is the corporeal plane, the AI will be the spirit in the ideal plane, and you the programmer will be the God of that universe you have created. The AI for sure is more than the series of 0s and 1s, it has the essence of intelligence given to them by you, the creator. If the AI is to study its simulated world, it'll find energy, order in term of the machine (the universe) and the code (laws), but if it was smart enough, it'll realize that there are more to it than that, yes, that essence of intelligence you gave it.

Now let's say you setup the system to select for some evolvable "useful" AI, after running the simulation, you select for the functional "smart" AI. Those will be selected to be placed in a much better supercomputer where they can unleash their true potentials. While any other AI that caused an error or was unable to evolve, you simply will delete it, or put it in another low level computer to confine it or repurpose it.

Now let's take this example one step higher. The source of all ideas (God) create the simulation or dream plane (the universe), for him we exist, and for us we also exist, we see the manifestations of God's ideas as dualities.

God's dream is our reality.

This might rings a bell with some physicists who advocates the holographic principle!

But remember you are not that same as your dream, as much as your dream or simulation is not you. In essence nor complexity.

So NO pantheism here.

Now coming back to this universal law of duality. We mentioned the infinite ultimate always present ideal plane, but what will be the opposite pair to that?

Of course, it is the ultimate nothingness, the zero. But by definition the ultimate nothingness, is nothing. It can never exist, or be at any moment. It has always never been and never will be. This automatically means the ultimate existence was always there and always will be.

Was this the simplest logical way to explain the ultimate infinite ideal plane? The source of all, God!

Wait a minute!
Too much talk and still you haven't answer the title of the book.

Why?
Sure I'll do…

But for a moment, let as contemplate something. Few elements, subatomic particles that differ in count and order is what makes me and you different from dirt. And a magical or a spiritual touch or whatever you want to call it…
And Boof!!!

Here we are, contemplating the universe. Not only

tangible things, but emotions, and above that absolute ideas, such as in math and philosophy.

Isn't that great by itself?

To understand, to be intelligent, to be free (even if partially).

I feel grateful for having these abilities.

Especially our ability to transcend the material plane and realize and comprehend the metaphysical.

But what all that has to do with the question 'why'.

Our Ability to Ask

That ability to question and to seek answers, mainly asking using "why" is the key to answer the reason of our existence.

Our ability to ask is the answer!
Am I not trying to escape from the answer?

No.
I'll explain...

To understand a meaning you have to experience it, live it and interact with it so it leaves its effect on you. For example, if you try to explain the meaning of dangers to a child, he will not understand it by mere verbal nor pictorial explanations. The only way he is going to understand the meaning of danger is when he experience danger. The child touches the fire match, ouch! That is painful, next time don't do it, it's dangerous. The child walked very fast on a wet floor then slipped, again, that's dangerous, etc...

To give a better example, can you explain the meaning of the color 'red' to a blind man? How are you even going to start?

-It's a color.
-What is a color?
-An effect of a light wave.
-What is light?

-An energy, which radiates from certain objects, then get reflected from the surface of other objects, to reach the sensors in our retina, then it transform into an electrochemical signal, which get transmitted to the brain, and somehow in that darkness over there, the consciousness gives it the meaning "red".

-Nice explanation…
But, I do not understand!
All these words means nothing to me.

Well, no matter how much you try it is all in vain.
A blind man can never understand the meaning of 'redness' unless he see it by himself.

This condition of an experience and personal interaction is a universal necessity to understand each and every meaning.

What is hunger? And what is satiety?
What is fear? And what is tranquility?
What is weakness? And what is strength?
What is justice? And what is prejudice?

You can never understand any of these meanings without

experiencing them, interacting with them on a personal level, where they can leave their effect on you.

Now...

The first and the only cause by logical necessity, the primary source of all these meanings, have brought to existence an entity that can understand meanings and comprehend ideas. But how can these intelligent beings learn? To know themselves? And to know their maker?

Someone might answer in a rush, well if God is that potent and wise, why didn't he made a being with all the meanings preprogrammed in its memory. So the being is created knowing all.

Yes, that indeed seems like an easy answer. Why all the hustle and bustle then?

But why didn't God opt for that method?

Well, because it does not work. It contradicts many of the ideas that the human has to understand, like: freedom and responsibility.

Some other ideas have to be experienced on a personal level, like: love, happiness, gratitude and relief. These ideas have to be acquired not given.

And finally, a silly reasoning you might think! There is more pleasure and satisfaction in learning by living the experience, gaining after loss and advancing from a lower level to a higher level of wisdom. To know the value of things you have to lose them first.

So, to give this intelligent being the chance to learn all these meanings, we have to place it in an environment where it can experience several examples or manifestations of each idea. Where the ideas can leave their effect on its consciousness for it to form (discover) the meaning.

And since we talked about the duality of each idea once it is manifested in what we call the universe. This training ground (school) has to allow for these opposite dualities to manifest.

Like any other school system, there are certain requirements to guarantee the delivery of the information from the teacher to the student:

1- Rules and tools to help the student to learn.
2- A time frame or schedule, to give the student a sense of progression, and direction.
3- An end to each learning stage, with a monitoring and evaluation system.
4- Depending on the evaluation, the student can advance to a higher level and access new knowledge.

I see that life on earth ticks all the boxes. This school we live in gives us the chance to understand ideas in their opposite dualities. There are hunger and satiety, weakness and strength, justice and prejudice, darkness and light, knowledge and ignorance, good and evil.

Every pair has its chance to manifest, to leave its impression on us at a personal level to help reveal the ultimate meanings. Since the gain always come after loss, we strongly realize the value of things. We value health after sickness, we value justice after prejudice, we value knowledge after ignorance, and of course we value existence after nothingness.

That is why I see no meaning in an original sin. It was an attempt to explain the existence of the "negative" pair gone wrong! There is no creation without the manifestation of the duality of meanings, because without dualities meanings will have no meanings.

What happened to Adam and Eve was only the beginning of the lesson (talking to those who adhere to Abrahamic religions). Simply Adam and Eve have stopped being toddlers who should be taking care of, acting without any real contemplation in the meaning of their actions. The moment of eating the fruit that God have forbid them to eat before, was actually a blessing. Finally those intelligent entities have matured and realized their power, that moment have generated several dualities: good and evil, punishment and forgiveness, innocence and responsibility.

In the Judeo-Christian belief, this moment has been portrayed in rather a negative narrative. Eve was tempted by the devil, then Eve was blamed more than Adam for tempting him to eat from the tree, God is angry at Eve and Adam, now they have the power of knowledge! All humanity is cursed, even the newborn child who is innocent, is a sinner! For a crime he never committed! No matter how much you apologize for it, you can't be forgiven! Unless somehow God had to be degraded to a man, then kill himself, then save himself! Then you are forgiven!

As I mentioned, I see this as a wrong attempt to explain the existence of the "negative" pair when ideas manifest as objective realities. The other Abrahamic religion, Islam on the other hand, mentioned the same event rather briefly without much details nor negativity, the narrative was more simple and easy going, simplified by me as the following:

God: Adam and Eve you can eat from all the trees in this garden where you are protected from heat, cold and hunger, except from one tree (nothing special really, just a tree).

Time had passed...

Evil: Bsst! Hey! Adam, Hey! Eve, do you know why God didn't want you to eat from that tree? If you don't eat you'll be angels and if you do eat you'll become immortal.

Well, if we recall that angels have bowed down for Adam -as a sign of his superiority- so definitely Adam don't want to be an angel!

That made the other option more logical in their brain.
Adam and Eve ate from the tree...
They became adults, first dualities manifested: innocence-responsibility.

God: Why did you disobey my orders? I told you the devil is your enemy.

Adam: Sorry, I didn't imagine he would say something that is not true (lie).

God: I forgive you.
Tutorial ends now.

Now the lesson of life on earth start for you and all humans after you.

End of story.

No anger, no eternal punishments, no blaming poor Eve, even no direct punishments for Satan himself! All was part of the school set up, a tutorial, if you prefer!

At that moment Adam and Eve learned the meaning of many ideas responsibility-innocence, forgiveness-punishment, truth-lies, friend-enemy, struggle-comfort, etc...

Now if you have the appetite for some critical thinking, it's up to you to decide which narrative is more digestible!

Now how can all that package of knowledge be considered bad or avoidable? Well it was not. We have been brought to existence to understand these meanings in the first place.

A moment please!

Now please don't call me an anti-Christian or anti-Judean or anti this or that. For questioning the original sin narrative leads to questioning the savior narrative, which leads to questioning the whole Judeo-Christian dogma! I am only asking questions. Don't we have the right to ask?

Believe me if I wanted to have any aggressive approach I would have started with more challenging questions like: Why God chose the progeny of one man and elevated them above all the other humans? Isn't that racist? What God would do such a thing! Did God actually do that? By asking these questions I am not an anti-Semite, I even object on the use of the word 'Semite' which is a racist definition by definition. And by the way you cannot be 'anti-me' then when I complain about that, you label me as 'anti-you'! I am a gentleman otherwise I would have followed that remark with a curse word.

Also, I advocate for changing the notion of Semitic languages, to be based on geographical presence or place of origin as in Indo-European. Thus, we can use Afro-Arabian based on spread and origins in Arabian Peninsula and Africa, or go larger as in Afro-Asiatic or smaller as in Mesopotamian, North & South-Arabian, North-African, etc. This practice is the standard in linguistic studies, except for the Afro-Arabian branch where a religious reference is used instead! Now you can already see how religious this description is when calling the other language families Hamitic and Japhetic. Again, forcing the majority of the world to accept a Judeo-Christian narrative. I still recall that linguistics is a science…

For when accepting the -religious- narrative of one group of people and force it on all humanity as facts this feeds the superiority complex that they have! I also recall, we had similar groups who claimed supremacy above other fellow humans based on nationality and birthright!

Now are such logic either constructive or welcomed worldwide? Just asking.

Also, since we have opened this discussion. It's rather funny to base your superiority on the number of prophets and messengers that were sent to you. Now if you have two students that have to learn the same lesson. You hired a teacher to teach them, the first student learned the lesson directly, the other student didn't. So you hired another teacher, then another, then another. Now which one of the students has a problem? Again, just asking!

To summarize, I simple argue that we are all equal in humanity. No superior "race". This is silly! Come on.

Nor I will start with questions regarding an omnipotent omniscient God, pictured as a giant running around in heaven searching for Adam and Eve after they have "sinned"! Nor the six thousand years old earth, nor the creation of plants before the sun! Nor that until the creation of man earth had not seen any rain! ETC… All these questions -after just few pages in the scripture- would be more challenging for the adopted narrative in current dogmas.

This is the difference of a scientific, logical, critical reading of the claimed "holy" textures. (Please always read like this).

But Again…

You see how slippery that was, I don't want to enter in a religious debate on what is right and what is wrong? What are truths and what are lies? This is not the aim of such book, here we merely are interested in asking existential questions, all questions without limitations. Then we simply showcase what some philosophies offer as answers, then we briefly contemplate the logic behind them. Finally, we follow a logical critical scientific approach in answering these questions, to reach the explanation with the highest probability of being true or real.

And I have questions for all philosophies and dogmas known to humans. For those who believe in many Gods when their book is stressing that there is only one, to those who think of God in a pathetic degenerative way as a human with some superpower, to those who go on a kill spree to force their dogmas, to those who isolate themselves in the name of wisdom! To those credulous individuals who have a naive superiority complex. And questions to those who advocated complete equality of results (not opportunities) in naturally hierarchical societies and claim a permanent -false-divinity of the masses, then call it a "commun"-sense. And questions to those who reduced the whole complexity and beauty in the universe to nothingness! To those and those and all.

It's a very long list of questions that goes on and on…

Now you, I and everyone else are free to adhere to any belief system they find comfortable. We've made that clear in the previous pages! I only wish that this comfort is based on logic and wisdom rather than ethnocultural influence or socio-historical indoctrination.

After this explanatory detour, let's go back again to our main question "why this universal routine?"

The answer from the aforementioned logical analysis is:
We live -the routine- to understand meanings and comprehend ideas.

It's a routine, so everybody has more or less the same chance to experience all ideas, in line with the principles of equal opportunities, justice & equality for all, etc.

We are alive now to learn, to value what we have, to be free and responsible, to learn how to control ourselves, to choose the right things according to our conscious free well, to dwell in the plane of the ideal above the materialistic objective manifestations.

Now that what is meant by being a God-like.

But this life (routine) is hard and boring!
Also there is too much evil in this world!
Well it should be, remember it's a duality. Both pairs must manifest.

Also, good and evil are relative terms. Since you are not God, you are an incomplete being by default and you have weaknesses. Hence, any action that reveal these weaknesses and put your existence in jeopardy, you label it evil. The spider web is good for the spider, but evil for the butterfly. Goodness and evilness are but a duality of the one idea manifestation.

I too don't like seeing many mistakes get repeated over and over again through the course of humanity's journey on earth. You wish that everybody are wise and smart in their actions and reactions. But alas!

Maybe this too is part of the learning process!

To be patient, to learn not to hate the other, even when they behave in utter stupidity! Nor hate yourself if you do that too! Maybe you should learn to sympathies and extend your helping hand, try to be a benevolent force.

Or maybe it is only a selfish act derived by personal gain and ego satiation. Now I see what stupidity and ignorance lead to, I value wisdom. I feel bad for those who lost it, I feel good for those who are searching for it, and I feel ardent to reach those who gained it.

Anyhow, this training period is rather brief. For the clock arms should be going backward in a countdown. As students who are waiting for the exam time to finish. Some students don't feel the time passing since they are too busy reading the study material and trying to answer the questions, other students are busy with the decoration of the classroom, others are busy arguing if the books are original copies or not, others just shouting and distracting their fellow students, others are fighting on the "best" chair in the classroom! And they've forgotten the purpose of the whole thing. And very few others have already finished the reading material available, answered all the questions on the examination paper, and now they are just setting there bored of waiting, looking at the other students struggling! And contemplating the next stage after the evaluation is to be made.

If you are intelligent and smart, you have patience and self-control, and if you are logical and wise in your approach, you will ask these existential questions and attempt to answer them. Now you might reach many of the answers without much help from the outside. But you and I know very well, that humans vary in their attitude, living, logic, heritage, etc. Which leads to people be more or less interested in pursuing such mentally challenging philosophical activities with a high level of logical fairness, due to socio-historical prior built paradigms, heritage and religious beliefs, lack of access to knowledge, lack of the capacity to understand the knowledge (time, language, etc.), and more dominantly the lack of motivation due to their over emersion in the daily universal routine itself.

That's why during the course of humanity's journey on earth, there have been those selected few who had the task of reminding the busy masses of the reason of existence and the meaning of everything.

Those wise men could only remind people, rekindle the flame of love of wisdom (philosophy) in them. They have the task to explain what was mystified, to clean what was tarnished by ignorance and misconception, to remove the veils that people cover themselves with so they can finally see the absolute ultimate truth.

Some did it because of their moral awareness, they might have been self-motivated, hoping to live in a rational society. Others in addition to their self-motivation had received help from the original teacher and the first reason (God), to expand their task to larger masses. We called them gurus, prophets and messengers.

Their task was to correct the wrongness in human societies, to explain the meaning again, to deliver the same message again and again: there is a meaning to your existence, know thyself and know thy maker, use your power to question and understand, don't be automatic, just another animal driven by instinct and material needs. Don't fully immerse yourself in matter and forget what really matters!

A small note to be mentioned. With all respect to these enlightened humans, they were indeed humans. The sanctification of these individuals was not needed, as in elevating them to Godhood status! Let me give you this example, If you were a ruler of a small town, and you wanted to send a message to the King or Emperor, you call a messenger who is clever, faithful and honest, you give him a nicely eloquently written letter, then make sure the messenger is dressed well and equipped with all that he needs to deliver the message. Now imagine you wanted to send another message to your warden to bring a criminal to be judged, well you might as well just ask some little kid to go fetch him. Now why this example? To show that the importance of the messenger depends on the receiver. So, God's messengers were honored and important because they were sent to us. God chose the best to deliver his message because humans are rather an important creature. This makes you think, why we are important to deserve such treatment?

Now with the change in time period, geographical place, level of accumulated knowledge, with the unity of the message, the teaching method was adapted to best suits the capacities of each society.

So, in simple more primitive societies -not looking down on them, just highlighting the lack of accumulated knowledge they had- the teaching method was more direct and tangible. For hunter gatherer societies, having food for example was a major concern, it was not an easy task, and once they hunt an animal they have to eat it or preserve it for the days when they couldn't hunt. So the messenger will try to free them from this over immersion in their routine. Thus, a worship would've been some form of material sacrifice (an animal, fruits, etc.) to teach them that they are not predatory animals, they eat to live not live to eat, to learn that they are better, they can choose, they are in control of these materialistic impulses.

Of course people will not believe anyone who claim to have a divine message without a proof. An act that clearly show the superiority of the source, to avoid charlatans and imposters. So, the first teachers came with proofs that suited and challenged the norms in their time period, more materialistic tangible feats, like walking on water, not burning by fire, amplifying the few, or resurrecting the dead, etc.

But with the advancement of humanity, the teaching method started to get more and more intellectual rather than physical. Hence the last of the great religions was highly intellectual.

Wait, wait!!

Science, logic and religion!
Aren't they in conflict with each other?

Well, yes and no.

By science I mean the natural sciences, and by religion I mean the metaphysical 'spiritual' philosophies.

As I said before, nobody should deny the beauty and strength of the scientific method. Starting with observing, then questioning, then hypothesizing, and experimenting, then analyzing, and finally believing.

But aren't there a clear contradiction between science and religion?

Well of course there is...

Firstly, science is not absolute, it is changeable. What is true today could be proven false tomorrow. On the other hand, most religions are absolute, final, with not room for change.

Secondly, science excel in answering the question 'how', while religion focus on answering the 'why'.

And finally, science is precise and clear, while religion usually reach us with a lot of ambiguity. This is usually due to several reasons such as: textures that are written in an original ancient language are lost -while translations can never be 100% accurate- and their content is susceptible to addition or omission (human errors).

This susceptibility to change was the major problem that have faced religions from antiquity to modern days. For every generation change the original information (exact text) by rephrasing, addition or omission. Sometime with good intentions, to explain or simplify, etc. Other times with a mischievous intentions, to achieve a material gain or monopoly of power and knowledge. And some other times this change happen unintentionally, due to the passage of time and the lack of proper record keeping.

And when such changes occur in a religion, it appear wrong and in contradiction with itself, logic and nature, to those who come later in time. Well sure it must! We are detecting the human error here, imagine a priest adding or rephrasing the original scripture that is talking about a natural phenomenon, he will do it with the capacities of that era, which might be quite humble and often wrong. Now, by adding his opinion as part of the original text, this creates a problem for us now when we look at the scripture, we see contradictions and primitive thinking. That's why many well educated people refuse many religions. It is mainly due to these human errors happened in the past.

But even though science and religion appear to be in an irreconcilable conflict, in the end both are philosophies. A method of inquiry and critical thinking ending in belief. The difference is that the scientific belief is supported by measurements and experiments, always under the test for possible falsification, and only the highest possible chance is considered a truth (usually).

But can't we apply this scientific method to religion?
Sure we can, after all it is an intellectual activity.

As a scientist, it is almost impossible for me to believe something only by the word of the mouth, by stories! I want something that I can examine, I want a proof that can withstand the many falsification attempts, and I need more than one, and only when the test result all agree on the truthfulness of that information, I might believe.

So what about religions?
Every religion came up with a set of ideas, a narrative, a scripture that explain the metaphysical philosophy and mention the physical universe. Can't we put these religious theories to test then?
Well I don't see why not!

Let's exclude those metaphysical philosophies that do not claim they are from a divine source. For simply if there are errors there, they are human errors, and no human is perfect. Sometimes we get it right other time we don't.

But what I really want to test are those metaphysical philosophies that claim a divine origin. Those should be error free. For God is perfect.

Many followers of such religions would quickly reply: "but the prophet of this religion has proved its divine origin, haven't you read about all the miracles he performed?".

Ah! You mean those physical miracles!

Maybe!

But I was not there to see it with my own eyes. Maybe I would've believed him if I was there! But your prophet is long gone, and I am sorry because I can't build my belief on stories. I am not denying it by the way, but I need other proof that I can test. Otherwise what the prophet came with will only work for people at his time period.

Mmm, what about the book?
This book is from God.

Nice, now this is much better. Something tangible that I can examine. This will be the religious theory. Now let's see if it will withstand the test.

In scriptures, there are several things mentioned:

1- The universe and its creation, a mention of some key natural phenomena.
2- Description of the creation of life, especially humans.
3- A mention of some past and future events.
4- A mention of the best social system that the humanity should follow to live happily, peacefully, etc.

But there is more! I know, like morals, maxims, rites and worship etc. But that is not suitable to use for judging the divinity of your source, for any human could come up with a set of moral codes gathered from here and there, as we mentioned before, we all have some residual morality even on the subconscious level. But the four aforementioned points are better criteria for judging the divinity of the source. Let's take them one by one.

The universe and its creation, a mention of some key natural phenomena:

Simply, if the scripture claims that the universe was created from the body of a dead god, or his vomit tear or any other bodily fluid! Or if it mention that we all live on the back of a turtle or an elephant, then I refuse it in an instant. As for the natural phenomena, if they are personified and turned into gods, then as we mentioned before this was the simplification done by some teachers, the comic book sort of explanation, sorry I have to refuse that too.

The religion has to be clear in mentioning that the universe started from a state of singularity then got differentiated then expanded. Before stars and planets there were gas clouds, all objects are physical entities, not deities. Then earth came to being, a planet that went through different phases, it has different layers, moving tectonic plates then mountains, an atmosphere that protect the life.

And since we are talking about science, I would love to see some proof of the mathematical supremacy in the scripture.

But isn't that a lot to ask for from a religious scripture?

No, I even want more than that, and I don't want any wrong answers.

What about the creation of the living things, especially humans:

First, the religion has to mention that humanity came late to earth, it was not the first by any means and before it there were many other creatures that lived then got extinct, we didn't live as humans in the Cambrian era nor we strolled the earth with dinosaurs!

I want a logical chronological mention of the gradual creation of all these different organisms over millions of years, for the idea of creating things with a magick wand is refused, surely we don't see that in the universe now! I want a mention of life origin, dust and water "Mud!", the solution of life and the building material. This and more…

As for the mention of some past and future events:

What was a description of a past event, it is difficult to validate its accuracy, except it should not contradict our recent archaeological discoveries, nor logic. As for the description of future events (prophecies), there are two types: a past perfect prophecy, a prediction that had already happened in the past (it was a future for the people living with the prophet but now it is past for us), and a future prophecy which might happen in our future. These prophecies must be on a level that challenge the human capacity of prediction and intuition. In other words, what was presently available then should not be enough to make such predictions. This will highlight the superiority of the information source. For example: to predict when and how a person will die, or to predict the outcome of a war that has not started yet, or to predict a very specific natural event, etc. These prophecies have to be exact not ambiguous as in a great war will happen! Or a great king will die! Or a great wealth awaits you! Or there will be a great fire, storm, etc., for that is closer to a charlatan than to a prophet. Rather it should be exact as in that man or woman will die on that specific day, in this exact way! Or there will be a war between A and B, for this many years then A will emerge victorious, etc.

Now these kind of specific exact prophecies have a high risk of being falsified, and this is exactly why they can be considered a proof of a divine source. For if the man that the prophecy predicted his fortune or death in a very specific way dies in a different place or time, the whole faith in the fidelity of the prophet is in peril. Besides that, it will be very illogical for a prophet to challenge himself in this specific manner, where many things can go wrong! Why to do such a thing and risk being labeled as a liar and maybe risk being punished later by his own followers! Unless he is sure beyond doubt that this prophecy will come to be.

Finally, regarding the mention of the best social system that the humanity should follow to live happily, peacefully, etc.

Needless to say, it should have a code of morality, no cheating, stealing, killing or other actions the people in general are repugnant to. For even the biggest liar on earth hate to be lied to, nor does the biggest thief would like someone to steal his property. But as I said, many other earthly systems could come up with some similar moral code. But what they lack is another thing...

Justice.

Almost always the earthly systems are based on the benefit of one over the other. But the true religion should be clear about the equality between all humans, all must have equal chances to live, learn, move, think freely, etc. No superiority of the rich over the poor, children of kings over children of farmers, one color over the other, of people who live here on people who live there! No children of God and no chosen people.

The religious teachings must protect the weak, and do justice to the oppressed, it must define rulers as servant of the people, again no ruling as representatives of God, nor any monopoly of the truth in the hand of some hierarchy that speak in God's name. A true religion must not force the other to follow it, it must value freedom of choice and variation in society. It must guide the state to protect this freedom, maintain peace and make sure all is served equally.

Now any problem in the aforementioned conditions will be a sign of the scripture's earthly origin or the human error introduced into the divine teachings, by the hands of those who wrote the scriptures in antiquity.

But is there a religion like that?
Ticking all the boxes!
Sure, but again this is up to you to discover!

I have 0 interest in convincing you in any philosophy here, I really don't care what you end up choosing.

Sorry for being too honest!
For if you choose to be wise and critical in your life, you benefit yourself. And if you choose to cover your eyes, and let emotions and some ancestral indoctrination governs your life, you are harming yourself.

In general, it is natural that I wish all people choose to be wise, critical and scientific. To realize the power they possess, this ability to inquire and seek answers, to have a free choice and to be responsible.

I might write a book in the future discussing different philosophies or religions and their agreement with our current knowledge in the light of science and modern technologies. Which of them have withstood the challenge of falsification and the meticulous critical examination. But! All that will be in vain, if the individual don't want to have critical thinking, doubt or question everything he knows. For how many are still believing in a flat earth! Or a six thousand years old earth! Against all the facts that prove otherwise. Their eyes are open, but they cannot see!

It might be a form of arrogance! A pride in some inherited culture or some ancestral legacy (strangely accepting the slavery to the past!). Or it might be a refusal of the truth because they contradict with some materialistic gains (Ehm, money! Ehm, power!). But for me there are this one underlying reason. A source of all that is wrong, which is stupidity. For I see all mistakes as unintelligent -stupid-reactions. For if you are truly intelligent and wise you will never opt for a wrong action. And if you realize the routine and the absurdity of what generate all these conflicts, you will never let hatred, envy, deceit, greed, etc., dominate your life.

Again, we are not perfect, and we don't have ultimate wisdom, thus we make and see mistakes around us.

But at least it is a good thing to realize mistakes as mistakes, and work on avoiding them in the future as much as we could.

I hope we all make use of the intelligence we have. For "Why" is the most beautiful gift that we have ever received.

I hope we all opt for actions based on wisdom and true understanding, rather than some animalistic automatic reactions.

I hope we all believe in the 99.99..% not the near zero prediction, in a great conflict with basic logic.

I hope we keep asking and asking, until we reach that near 99.99..% prediction.

Then that we remember, it's a prediction, a very smart guessing, a fact that still have very tiny room for doubt.

Then to accumulate the doubts over each other, until they reach certainty. After a very long contemplation.

Then to remember that that is not yet the absolute holistic ultimate truth yet!

For many veils have to be lifted before we can truly see.

Ask about everything.
Everything.
Nothing is above or beyond questioning.
Ask and then believe, not the opposite.

Speaking about questions, I still believe you haven't answered the title of the book yet!

The Reason of Existence

We have already explored some of the human behavior and activities, on the individual level and on the society level. We searched for a meaning behind these actions, we explored some of the philosophies that have tried to give answers to these questions, especially those existential questions. We found that the materialistic philosophies more or less reached a conclusion that there is no meaning in asking 'why' just ask 'how'. Or simply and more bravely 'there is no meaning'.

As for those who find this materialistic belief not supported by a high level of certainty! Nor enough to explain many other phenomena such as consciousness, free will, beauty, order, etc. Those who can still sense the strength in their ability to ask, to doubt, to seek wisdom, they outbalance the logical necessity of God's presence.

As for the people who still think that there is no meaning of anything, well, again, it's very strange you reached that far in the book! What was the meaning of that?

Weird...Don't lie to yourself!
And as for those who are still searching for meanings, we show that life on earth might be a training session. An arena made for the absolute ideas to manifest in their dualities. That was our partial answer for 'why this universal routine?'.

But the question remains.
Why us?
Why is there creation in the first place?
Why doesn't God exist without any other creation?
Just him alone.
I said before, all questions, and nothing above inquiry.

We might answer in a hurry, well, he is God, God can create thus he created, or there has to be a creature out there all the time for him to be a creator.

Not really, for you can have an ability without manifesting it. For example, you can be innately honest, even in the absence of an event for you to manifest your honesty.

Also the presence of some creation does not answer why exactly heavens, earth and humans? What happens next? What will happen after this training session we call life ends?

Is it a promise of an eternal existence (immortality), with less materialistic restrictions! A promise of satisfaction and eternal euphoria! But why?

Did he created us to know him? To praise him? I don't think he needs that! Also, it is rather a selfish reason! Now if we see it as a selfish reason, for sure the perfect God see it as a selfish reason too, and he would have never intended to create us solely to praise him.

On the other hand, if it is us who benefit from knowing him, then that explains why we exist now, but not why did he created 'us' in the first place, and not something else.

Well, I am afraid my friend that we have reached our capacity now. Why the afterlife, why the universe, why God has created?

These are questions that we can justly ask, but I don't think that any human or other intelligent being ever lived or will ever live on earth or any other place in the universe can answer.

But there is a reason for that. The problem lies in the fact that God is infinite and unlimited and we are finite and limited. And we are really bad -at least now- in dealing with infinities, or with nothingness.

Firstly, this is due to our limited intellectual capacities in this life. Before jumping to the 'why', we are still struggling with the simpler 'how'. For example, for a little 3 years old kid, to know that ice is water in the solid state is an achievement, for that is his intellectual capacity limits at that age. Now the child grows up, he goes to school, then to university, to realize the physical laws behind the solid and liquid state of water (atoms ordered and vibrating according to temperature, pressure, etc.). Then he studies more to realize the subatomic particles and the fascinating quantum world, then he studies more, to the level where the particles disappear, and we are in front of energy fields manifesting in different ways. One more step and we jump into higher dimensions, mathematical equations start forcing us to think of a holographic simulated universe. The whole thing becomes complicated again as if he has entered a new infancy!

Indeed, for the road is still in its beginning.

Many of us have equipped ourselves with the necessary skills for any higher understanding. Elevated ourselves above the superficial materialistic manifestations, to contemplate the meaning in the ideal plane.

For all the vastness of the universe is smaller than 'why' answer.

The answer for 'why' cannot be delivered by messengers, nor written in books. For how many are the things that cannot be explained by words, exactly as our failed attempts to explain the meaning of a color to a blind man.

Now, what I can wish for is that you keep asking, searching for the truth, never give up or surrender to a total immersion in the materialistic routine, never lose your strength and control over your decisions.

I can only promise -rather courageously- that you will be satisfied walking that path, and when you reach your destination, you will obtain the ultimate euphoria. Now be aware of what you wish for and have patience.

For the difference between who aims wrong and who
aims right
Is as the difference between the brightest day and the
darkest night
Now, may love, wisdom and peace prevail
And may your eyes never be covered by any veil

About the Author

Tareq is a scientist, an activist, a writer and a blogger. He has a Ph.D in Biology from KU Leuven, and a M.Sc in Energy Science from Kyoto University. But before all, he considers himself a lover of wisdom 'a philosopher'.

www.ingramcontent.com/pod-product-compliance
Lightning Source LLC
Chambersburg PA
CBHW071904020426
42331CB00010B/2665